An Ignatian
Introduction to
Prayer

Other Books by the Author

THE EXAMEN PRAYER
Ignatian Wisdom for Our Lives Today

THE DISCERNMENT OF SPIRITS
An Ignatian Guide for Everyday Living

SPIRITUAL CONSOLATION
An Ignatian Guide for the Greater Discernment of Spirits

An Ignatian Introduction to
Prayer

Scriptural Reflections
According to the
Spiritual Exercises

TIMOTHY M. GALLAGHER, OMV

A Crossroad Book
The Crossroad Publishing Company
New York

The Crossroad Publishing Company
831 Chestnut Ridge Road
Chestnut Ridge, NY 10977

www.crossroadpublishing.com

Printed in the United States of America on acid-free paper

The text of this book is set in 11/15 Adobe Garamond.

Library of Congress Cataloging-in-Publication Data

Gallagher, Timothy M.
  An Ignatian introduction to prayer : spiritual reflections according to the Spiritual exercises / Timothy M. Gallagher.
    p. cm.
  Includes index.
  ISBN-13: 978-0-8245-2487-6 (alk. paper)
  ISBN-10: 0-8245-2487-X (alk. paper)
  1. Ignatius, of Loyola, Saint, 1491-1556. Exercitia spiritualia. 2. Christian life – Catholic authors. 3. Spiritual exercises. I. Title.
  BX2179.L8G35 2008
  248.3 – dc22

                                                                    2007046625

6 7 8 9 10   A   16 15 14 13 12

Contents

A Word Regarding This Book

This is a book for those who desire to pray with Sacred Scripture. It is a book to be *used* for prayer.

I composed these reflections after years of presenting scriptural texts to retreatants in the Ignatian Spiritual Exercises. In keeping with Ignatius of Loyola's counsel, I have limited them to brief thoughts, simple suggestions, which the reader is invited to develop in personal prayer.

For those beginning to pray with Scripture, these reflections may serve as accompaniment in the first, tentative steps of such blessed prayer. For those who already pray with Scripture, and who seek new depth in that prayer, they may provide an opportunity for such growth.

Spiritual directors may offer them to persons who desire to learn Ignatian meditation and contemplation — the reflective and imaginative approaches to prayer that Ignatius teaches, and which are employed in this book. These reflections may also assist retreat directors in proposing scriptural texts to retreatants, individually and in group settings — a simple means of providing, together with the text itself, brief suggestions for prayer with that text. In fact, these forty texts follow the outline of Ignatius's Spiritual Exercises. Finally, these reflections may serve as a basis for prayerful sharing by groups in parishes, among friends, in the home, or in similar gatherings.

May these pages assist those who use them to grow in love of the God whom their hearts seek.

* 1 *

BARTIMAEUS

Mark 10:46–52

"What do you want me to do for you?"

Scripture Reading

As I begin, I become aware of the Lord present to me,
looking upon me with love, desirous of speaking to my heart . . .

Prayerfully, I read Mark 10:46–52.

Meditation

I see the crowds, the road as it leaves the city, the blind beggar seated by the road . . . I am there with him . . . perhaps I take his place, and, now, I am seated there, like him, waiting . . .

He seeks to come to Jesus out of his great need, and his hope that in Jesus he will find healing. But he is helpless to approach the Lord . . . I sense my own need, my own hope, my own helplessness.

I watch as he pours out his need and his hope in the repeated cry: "Jesus, Son of David, have mercy on me!" His cry becomes the cry too of my heart: "Jesus . . . have mercy on me!" I make this prayer to the Lord . . .

Jesus hears this cry. He stops. He says to the crowd: "Call him." I hear them say to me: "Take heart; rise, he is calling you." I feel my heart begin to lift with new hope . . .

I stand before Jesus. Our eyes meet . . . I see his face, I hear his words, his question to my heart: "What do you want me to do for you?" Now Jesus and I are alone in the midst of the crowd. And I speak to him from my heart, unhurriedly. I dare to tell him all that I hope he will do for me...all that I hope for from this time of prayer...

I say to him: "Master, let me receive my sight." Help me to see! Help me see my way clearly in the doubts and fears that my heart feels; help me to overcome the obstacle that keeps me from the closeness I desire with you...

And, with Bartimaeus, I experience Jesus' word of healing...I sense the love that pours out from him and brings healing, brings new hope into my life...

I follow him along the way...

After the Prayer

- ◆ *What word in this Scripture most spoke to my heart?*
- ◆ *What touched my heart in this time of prayer? What did my heart feel as I prayed?*
- ◆ *What did I sense the Lord saying to me?*

* 2 *

EVERY ONE WHO THIRSTS

Isaiah 55:1–13

"Come, buy wine and milk / without money and without price."

Scripture Reading

*As I begin, I become aware of the Lord present to me,
looking upon me with love, desirous of speaking to my heart . . .*

Prayerfully, I read Isaiah 55:1–13.

Meditation

"Every one who thirsts, / come to the waters . . ." I hear the Lord speak these words to me. I tell the Lord of the thirsting of my heart: thirst for meaning, thirst for love, thirst for closeness with him, with others. I tell the Lord of the loneliness my heart experiences, of my sense of insufficiency . . .

And I hear the Lord say now to me: If your heart thirsts, *come to the waters. . . .* Come to the waters of the Spirit, the waters of grace . . . the waters that alone can quench the deep thirsting of the human heart.

"Come, buy . . . / without money and without price." I hear these words of *pure invitation;* there is no need to have "achieved" something spiritually before I can dare to approach. All that is necessary is to *come* and to receive God's gift.

"Why do you spend . . . / your labor for that which does not satisfy?" Lord, there are so many answers to your question: because I am confused, because I am afraid, because the effort to possess what truly satisfies seems too hard. . . . The Lord simply answers me: "Come . . ."

"And I will make with you an everlasting covenant, / my steadfast, sure love . . ." Lord, I open my heart to your *everlasting* covenant, your *steadfast, sure,* love . . . a bond of belonging and a love that will never fail . . .

"My thoughts are not your thoughts . . ." "As the heavens are higher than the earth, / so are my ways higher than your ways." My thoughts see so little . . . Your thoughts see so much more, your ways are beyond what I can grasp. Lord, I entrust myself to your thoughts and to your ways, to the mystery of your providence in my life.

The rain and the snow water and make fruitful the earth . . . "So shall my word be that goes forth from my mouth; / it shall not return to me empty." I open my heart to the power of that word, even now, as I pray with this Scripture. . . . Lord, fill my emptiness too with the nourishment of your word . . .

Now my prayer becomes quiet, deep, receptive . . . A silent gratitude wells up within me for the gift of your word that I meditate, Lord, and for its power to renew my life.

After the Prayer

- *What word in this Scripture most spoke to my heart?*

- *What touched my heart in this time of prayer? What did my heart feel as I prayed?*

- *What did I sense the Lord saying to me?*

JESUS' WORDS OF INVITATION

Matthew 11:25–30

"Come to me, all you who labor . . ."

─── *Scripture Reading* ───

As I begin, I become aware of the Lord present to me,
looking upon me with love, desirous of speaking to my heart . . .

Prayerfully, I read Matthew 11:25–30.

─── *Meditation* ───

I sense the thrill of gratitude in the heart of Jesus as he lifts up his heart to the Father whom he so loves, and by whom he knows himself so deeply loved . . . that same Father who says to me, as to Jesus: You are my beloved son, my beloved daughter . . .

Jesus thanks his Father that he has revealed the mysteries of the Kingdom not to the self-sufficient . . . but to those who feel themselves helpless, dependent on God for everything, like a small infant . . . I ask to be such . . .

I ask Jesus, the Son who knows the Father, to reveal himself, to reveal the Father to me, in this time of prayer . . . that he chooses to do this in my heart . . .

Now he is close to me, speaking to my heart. I hear his invitation: "Come to me . . ." I share with the Lord my own desire, now, in this time of prayer. Even as I sense my heartfelt longing to "come to him," to know that my heart is close to him . . . I hear him say to me, with infinite love: I want you to come close, I invite you, I call you, "Come to me . . ."

"You who labor and are heavily burdened...I will give you rest." Lord, grant me the rest that my restless heart so seeks. I embrace this invitation. I come to the Lord bringing my burdens, my heart's laboring and weariness. I hear his promise of rest, heart's rest...

"Take my yoke upon you and learn from me...for I am gentle and lowly of heart." Two words. Lord, you are *gentle,* you are *lowly* of heart. I ponder each word...There is no more room for fear...

"Learn from me." I ask the Lord for this "learning" in these times of prayer.... This is the learning my heart most desires: personal learning, relational learning, learning of Jesus... "And you will find rest for your souls. For my yoke is easy, and my burden is light." "You have made us for yourself, O Lord, and our hearts are restless, until they rest in you" (St. Augustine). I seek the Lord, I seek his rest...

After the Prayer

+ *What word in this Scripture most spoke to my heart?*
+ *What touched my heart in this time of prayer? What did my heart feel as I prayed?*
+ *What did I sense the Lord saying to me?*

JEREMIAH'S WORD OF HOPE

Jeremiah 29:11–14

"I know the plans I have for you."

Scripture Reading

As I begin, I become aware of the Lord present to me,
looking upon me with love, desirous of speaking to my heart...

Prayerfully, I read Jeremiah 29:11–14.

Meditation

I read the word of God, through the prophet Jeremiah, to his people in their time of exile.

Their hearts are heavy... Their nation, their temple, all that was dear to them, has been destroyed, and they are reduced to a helpless group of exiles, far from their home. The present is dark; the future, too, seems without hope, and their exile continues... My heart, too, knows such times...

And in their hearts, in our hearts, is fear — fear that this has happened through our own fault, through our failure to love and serve the Lord as we were called to do...

My heart too is afraid... I too fear that I am not what I ought to be, that I fail the Lord... Even in this time of prayer... will I respond to the Lord?

The Lord speaks to them... and the Lord speaks personally to my heart, here, in this moment of prayer.

"I know the plans I have for you ... plans for welfare and not for evil, to give you a future and a hope." I feel my anxieties about the future, about what lies ahead for me, about what will happen in my spiritual life, my prayer ...

I know that my desire to grow in love is real, but I feel so weak, so helpless ... and I am afraid. But now I hear this word of the Lord to me: "I know the plans I have for you ... " I hear these words deeply, I read them, I reread them ...

"You will call upon me and come and pray to me, and I will hear you." My heart lifts at this promise: "and I will hear you." Lord, now, today, I call upon you, I come to you, I pray to you ...

"You will seek me and find me." I speak to the Lord of my greatest desire: I seek you ... My heart opens as I hear your promise to me: and you will find me ...

"I will restore your fortunes ... " A new hope ... that my heart can truly change, can truly heal, can truly grow in love: "I will restore ... "

My heart lifts up as I hear the Lord speak these words personally to me ... offering me new hope, new trust, as I live my calling in his service, as I look to what lies ahead ...

I linger over these words, I read them, I hear the Lord speak to me. My heart responds.

After the Prayer

+ *What word in this Scripture most spoke to my heart?*
+ *What touched my heart in this time of prayer? What did my heart feel as I prayed?*
+ *What did I sense the Lord saying to me?*

FEAR NOT

Isaiah 43:1–7

"You are precious in my eyes, / and honored, and I love you"

Scripture Reading

*As I begin, I become aware of the Lord present to me,
looking upon me with love, desirous of speaking to my heart . . .*

Prayerfully, I read Isaiah 43:1–7.

Meditation

God speaks to the heart of the exiled people . . . and to me.

I sense the Lord with me, speaking these words to me. I read them slowly, tasting them, allowing their meaning to enter into my soul . . . I stay with the words that most speak to me, without hurry . . .

"Thus says the Lord, he who created you . . . he who formed you . . ." With the people of Israel, I again become aware of God at the origin of my being, of my belonging to his people. I sense the mystery of an eternal love that surrounds my whole being, my beginning, my life . . .

"Fear not": the word so often repeated by Jesus. I speak to the Lord of the fears in my heart: of my inadequacy, my failures, my slowness to respond . . . Again and again I hear his word: "Fear not."

"For I have redeemed you." I am your protector, I am at your side, I am with you; you are not alone. My power and my love accompany you . . . I hear the Lord speak his words to me . . .

"I have called you by name, you are mine." I think now of my own name. I hear the Lord pronounce my name, giving me my identity, giving me life, making me his own, telling me that I am not alone... In the silent depth of my heart, I hear the Lord pronounce my name... again, again... I respond...

"When you pass through the waters I will be with you; / and through the rivers, they shall not overwhelm you; / when you walk through fire, you shall not be burned": the symbol of the most dangerous situations, situations which threaten life itself... and these will be powerless to harm me. I will keep you unharmed even in the most difficult situations in life... A new trust dawns in my heart...

"Because you are precious in my eyes, / and honored, and I love you." Three words. With deep attention I ponder each: you are *precious* in my eyes; you are *honored* in my eyes; I *love* you. I dare to hear the Lord say these words to his people Israel... and to me...

Now my heart replies to the Lord who speaks his love to me...

After the Prayer

- *What word in this Scripture most spoke to my heart?*
- *What touched my heart in this time of prayer? What did my heart feel as I prayed?*
- *What did I sense the Lord saying to me?*

* 6 *

GOD AT THE ORIGIN OF MY BEING

Psalm 139:1–18

"You knit me in my mother's womb."

Scripture Reading

As I begin, I become aware of the Lord present to me,
looking upon me with love, desirous of speaking to my heart…

Prayerfully, I read Psalm 139:1–18.

Meditation

This psalm is a prayer, words spoken from the human heart to God. I make these words my own. I say them to the God who is present to me now…

A psalm of wonder, of marveling *at the closeness of God to me:* "You have searched me and known me!" My heart ponders this marvel, that the infinite and eternal God *knows me,* that I am important to him…

"You know when I sit and stand; / you understand my thoughts. … Even before a word is on my tongue, / Lord, you know it all." Again this sense of marvel, that God is so intimately close to me, always, faithfully, sharing with me the hidden depths of my heart, my hopes, my struggles, my thoughts…I invite him into my heart…

"Behind and before you encircle me / and rest your hand upon me…" His loving and protecting hand is always with me…No matter where I am, "your hand will guide me, / your right hand holds me fast." You are faithfully with me, at all times, in all the places of my life…

A psalm of wonder, of marveling now at God's eternal love, *calling me into being:* "You knit me in my mother's womb." I sense the Love that lies at the origin of my being, that gave me life, that gives me life each day, that tells me that I am valued and loved...

My heart speaks now to the Lord: "I praise you... / wonderful are your works." Gratitude awakens in my heart. My heart sings its wonder, its praise, to my God...

"How precious to me are your designs, O God." Here, in my prayer, I ponder the loving designs of God. They become precious to me anew; they give me hope, a sense of the meaning of my life.

I read, I reread, the words of this Psalm, allowing God to show me their meaning...

And now my heart replies to the Lord...

After the Prayer

- *What word in this Scripture most spoke to my heart?*
- *What touched my heart in this time of prayer? What did my heart feel as I prayed?*
- *What did I sense the Lord saying to me?*

CALLED FROM BEFORE MY BIRTH

Jeremiah 1:4–19

"Before you were born I consecrated you."

Scripture Reading

*As I begin, I become aware of the Lord present to me,
looking upon me with love, desirous of speaking to my heart...*

Prayerfully, I read Jeremiah 1:4–19.

Meditation

God speaks to Jeremiah's heart, and reveals to him the eternal love and plan that gave him life, and gives meaning to his life. Now he speaks to me...and shares this same message...

I listen to this grace-filled dialogue between God and Jeremiah. I hear God say these same words to me: "Before I formed you in the womb I knew you, / ...I consecrated you; / ...I appointed you." My spiritual gaze lifts to the eternal Triune God...within whose eternity I was known, loved, chosen, given a mission, a purpose in life...Now my heart speaks to my God...

His words to Jeremiah, to me, renew in me a sense of the origin of my being, of the meaning of my life, of the call to say "yes" to God's plan for my life. My hearts speaks its "yes" to this love, to this plan...

Jeremiah feels too weak to respond to the Lord's call: "I do not know how to speak...I am only a youth..." My heart too says: I do not know how, I am capable of so little, so much less than I sense you ask of me...

The Lord simply replies: "Do not say, 'I am only a youth.'... Be not afraid... for I am with you to deliver you." I hear him speak these words to me... Do not focus on your lack of strength, on your lack of human resources. "Be not afraid." "I am with you." New hope, new desire, arises in my heart...

"I make you this day a fortified city, an iron pillar, and bronze walls... For I am with you, says the Lord, to deliver you." Three images of God's faithful, protecting love, as I live my call... Each image speaks to me... "I am with you..."

Do I, like Jeremiah, feel inadequate to respond fully? I express my anxieties to the Lord, and I hear him tell me, too, that his strength, his presence will be enough...

I thank God for the gift of my life. I ask him for the grace I need to respond, without hesitation, in the way I live each day, to his eternal love and eternal plan for my life.

In the quiet of my prayer, my heart becomes still. A sense of an eternal love for me fills me... I speak in silence, from my heart, to the One who loves me...

After the Prayer

- *What word in this Scripture most spoke to my heart?*
- *What touched my heart in this time of prayer? What did my heart feel as I prayed?*
- *What did I sense the Lord saying to me?*

PARENT AND CHILD

Hosea 11:1–9; Isaiah 49:13–16

"When Israel was a child, I loved him."

Scripture Reading

As I begin, I become aware of the Lord present to me,
looking upon me with love, desirous of speaking to my heart...

Prayerfully, I read Hosea 11:1–9 and Isaiah 49:13–16.

Meditation

Hosea 11:1–9

In this text God speaks, telling the story of his love for his people, a love that is greater than the infidelities of his people, a love that overcomes anger, a love that is unshakably faithful...and we are listeners as he speaks...as he intends us to be. He is speaking about his love for me...

"It was I who taught Ephraim to walk, / I took them up in my arms...I led them with cords of compassion, / with the bands of love...I bent down to them and fed them..."

"How can I give you up...My heart recoils within me, / my compassion grows warm and tender..."

I read this text with my heart, slowly, allowing the Lord to speak to me personally, lingering unhurriedly upon the words that speak most to my heart...I read, I reread...My heart listens...

Isaiah 49:13–16

A mother's love...

"Zion said: 'The Lord has forsaken me; / my Lord has forgotten me.'" Lord, at times I too feel forsaken, forgotten...

"Can a woman forget her infant, / be without tenderness for the child of her womb?" I hear your answer. I think of a mother's love for her infant...This love speaks to me of a greater and even more unshakeable love...

"Even should she forget, / I will never forget you." I *will never* forget you...

"See, upon the palms of my hands I have written your name." You — your name, your needs, your life — are written on the palms of my hands, are ever in my heart...

I sense the Lord calling me to trust in his love for me, a love that is not shaken by my weakness...a love that never forsakes, never forgets.

Again, I read slowly, attentively, with my heart...

After the Prayer

◆ *What word in this Scripture most spoke to my heart?*

◆ *What touched my heart in this time of prayer? What did my heart feel as I prayed?*

◆ *What did I sense the Lord saying to me?*

POTTER AND CLAY

Jeremiah 18:1–6

"Like the clay in the potter's hand, so are you in my hand."

Scripture Reading

*As I begin, I become aware of the Lord present to me,
looking upon me with love, desirous of speaking to my heart…*

Prayerfully, I read Jeremiah 18:1–6.

Meditation

I have heard the Lord speak to me of his faithful love for me, calling me into being, giving a purpose to my life. Now a hope, a desire arises in my heart to respond with complete availability to God's call — like many before me, like Mary: "Behold, I am the handmaid…"

I hear the Lord call me, as he does Jeremiah, to go down to the potter's house. I go, I see the potter seated at his work place, with his potter's wheel, with the clay he takes in his hand.

I watch him mold the clay, unmake the vessel and reshape it anew, as seems best to him. I note the total availability of the clay in his hands, ready to be shaped as he chooses.

"Behold, like the clay in the potter's hand, so are you in my hand…"

I spend unhurried time with the potter, I watch him work, shaping, reshaping. …I let this image speak to me of God at work in my life, over the years, now, shaping, reshaping…

I ask the grace to be available to this divine action, to place no obstacles, to be ready to be shaped as the Lord chooses, the Lord who loves me: in situations of health, of work, in relationships, in the changes and unforeseen events of my life...

I enter deeply into the heart of Jesus, who, upon entering the world, says to the Father whom he loves: "Sacrifices and offerings you have not desired, / but a body you have prepared for me...Then I said, 'Behold, I have come to do your will, O God...'" (Heb 10:5–7).

"Behold, I have come to do your will, O God": these are the words that guide Jesus' entire life and mission. I offer my own will now to the Lord. I ask the grace to be more open, more like clay in the hands of the divine potter...I too now say with Jesus: "I have come to do your will..."

After the Prayer

◆ *What word in this Scripture most spoke to my heart?*

◆ *What touched my heart in this time of prayer? What did my heart feel as I prayed?*

◆ *What did I sense the Lord saying to me?*

SAYING "YES" TO GOD

Genesis 22:1–19

"God…said to him, 'Abraham!' And he said, 'Here am I.' "

— *Scripture Reading* —

As I begin, I become aware of the Lord present to me,
looking upon me with love, desirous of speaking to my heart…

Prayerfully, I read Genesis 22:1–19.

— *Meditation* —

"After these things God tested Abraham" — a test that will lead to an outpouring of blessings…

I live with Abraham this moment when God asks of him what is dearest to his heart, and Abraham is ready to say "yes" to God, even in this…

How ready am I to say "yes" to all that the Lord may be asking of me now? To his call to relinquish something, to take some new step, that will lead me closer to him, that will help me respond more fully to his love for me, to his plan for me?

I marvel at the faith and availability to God that Abraham shows here. With a trusting heart, I ask God for that same faith, that same availability…

I am with Abraham when God calls him: "Abraham!" "Here am I." My heart too says, "Here am I," open to your call…

I sense all that stirs in Abraham's heart when God asks a sacrifice that touches the deep places in his heart: "your only son Isaac, whom you love."

And Abraham simply obeys...trusting in the faithful love of the God who asks this of him...

I watch the journey to the mount; I hear the question of his son, Isaac: "Behold, the fire and the wood; but where is the lamb...?" And Abraham's reply: "God will provide himself the lamb..."

On the mount, God again calls: "Abraham!" "Here am I." "Do not lay your hand on the lad..."

And God blesses the great availability of Abraham: "Because you have done this, and have not withheld your son...I will indeed bless you and...multiply your descendants as the stars of heaven..."

I ask God for the faith of Abraham, to remove all that keeps me from a new and deeper "yes" to his call to grow spiritually, to deepen in holiness, in union with him...

I ask his grace to see clearly the obstacles that hold me back, the places in my life where it is hard for me to offer, like Abraham, what I so deeply love, where I struggle to say "yes..."

And I ask his love, his grace, to say, in a new way, with new openness, my "yes" of availability...in all...

After the Prayer

- *What word in this Scripture most spoke to my heart?*
- *What touched my heart in this time of prayer? What did my heart feel as I prayed?*
- *What did I sense the Lord saying to me?*

SAYING "NO" TO LOVE

Genesis 3:1–24

"The man and his wife hid themselves from the presence of the Lord."

Scripture Reading

*As I begin, I become aware of the Lord present to me,
looking upon me with love, desirous of speaking to my heart...*

Prayerfully, I read Genesis 3:1–24.

Meditation

I have heard the Lord speak to my heart of his love for me.... Everything in me wants to be available, to respond with all my being. I take time now to ponder the only real obstacle to my response: our human capacity to say "no" to love — the reality of sin in the world.

I ponder this so that, with new understanding, I may turn to the Lord as my *Redeemer,* and receive afresh the healing gift of his merciful love, purifying me, turning "no" into "yes," deep in my heart...

I read this text slowly, almost as though it were the first time, living this tragic story of temptation, deception, sorrow... to see the nature of the obstacle to love so that, seeing it, I may be freed from it.

"Did God say, 'You shall not eat of any tree...?'" The first doubt of God's real love and care is subtly sown... The woman listens, answers, begins to fall into the deception... I too know these first beginnings...

"You will not die... You will be like God." Place yourself, not God's word, at the center: this is the way to life, to power... The woman — and I — listen...

Desire grows in the woman... "She took of its fruit and ate..." The choice for self apart from God has been made. Her choice now spreads to another: "and he ate" as well.

Now the consequences emerge: "Then the eyes of both were opened...": a simplicity is lost, fresh areas of temptation and struggle arise, a harmony is broken... the consequences of every human "no" to God's love...

They *hide from God* — afraid now to approach the only love which can give rest to their hearts, the love for which they — and I — are made. Now it becomes harder to draw near to Love...

Mutual blaming, divisions, arise: "The woman...gave me fruit...and I ate."

Pain enters the world: "in pain you shall bring forth children"; toil, sweat, labor, come into human experience: "in toil you shall eat." And death, on so many levels, comes into the world: "to dust you shall return."

But even in this moment, the *promise of redemption* is present (v. 15).... Now I stand before the Cross of Christ. I look to the crucified One, and see the infinite love which dies to set me free from this "no" to love. My heart opens in gratitude; I ask to be purified, to be set free from the obstacle to love...

After the Prayer

+ *What word in this Scripture most spoke to my heart?*
+ *What touched my heart in this time of prayer? What did my heart feel as I prayed?*
+ *What did I sense the Lord saying to me?*

DO I SAY "YES" TO LOVE?

1 Corinthians 13:4–7; Romans 7:15–25

"Love bears all things, believes all things, hopes all things…"

Scripture Reading

*As I begin, I become aware of the Lord present to me,
looking upon me with love, desirous of speaking to my heart…*

Prayerfully, I read 1 Corinthians 13:4–7 and Romans 7:15–25.

Meditation

Now I look at my own life: today, in recent weeks, in these past months. I look at my life with an open heart, asking the Lord to show me the truth that will set me free.

As I do this, the infinite love in the eyes of the Redeemer surrounds me with light and warmth…His love tells me of his desire to heal my heart, to give new freshness to my life…

1 Corinthians 13:4–7

I am with the Lord. I hear him speak these scriptural words to me. I stop at each word which describes love. I look at my own life in the light of this word: my personal life, my life in relationship with others, my work, my words, my choices…I speak of this with the Lord…

"Love is":

"patient" And I?

"kind" And I?

"not jealous" Am I?

"not . . . boastful" Am I?

"not arrogant" What of me?

"not . . . rude" Am I sensitive to others?

"does not insist on its own way" Do I?

"is not irritable" Am I?

"is not . . . resentful" Am I?

"does not rejoice at wrong but rejoices in the right" How do I respond to others' weaknesses?

"bears all things" Do I?

"believes all things, hopes all things" Do I continue to hope for growth in others?

"endures all things" Do I?

My heart turns to the love of the Redeemer . . . I make my prayer for healing . . .

Romans 7:15–25

St. Paul's words become mine too: I desire the good, and, so often, do just what I do not want to do . . . I sense, with him, my helplessness to love in the way I desire.

Like his, my heart turns to Jesus: "Who will deliver me . . . ? Thanks be to God through Jesus Christ Our Lord!"

My heart pours out to Jesus its prayer for newness. Already, like St. Paul, I feel gratitude arise in my heart . . .

After the Prayer

+ *What word in this Scripture most spoke to my heart?*

+ *What touched my heart in this time of prayer? What did my heart feel as I prayed?*

+ *What did I sense the Lord saying to me?*

A CRY OF UTTER SINCERITY

Psalm 51:1–19

"Create in me a clean heart, O God."

Scripture Reading
---

*As I begin, I become aware of the Lord present to me,
looking upon me with love, desirous of speaking to my heart . . .*

Prayerfully, I read Psalm 51:1–19.

Meditation

Now I turn to the Lord with a heartfelt plea. Like David (see the title to Psalm 51), I live this moment when my spiritual eyes suddenly see with clarity. Like David, I make no more excuses, I no longer try not to see . . .

And from the most sincere depth of my heart, like him, I turn to the Lord seeking healing, daring to hope for a new and purified heart, to be set free from my obstacles to love . . . to be given a new experience of the joy of healing.

I take up the words of this prayer, Psalm 51. I say them slowly to the Lord, pausing where my heart feels the need, repeating these words with sincerity, with hope, with trust in the love of the One with whom I speak . . .

"Have mercy on me, O God, / according to your merciful love." "Have mercy on me" . . . the mercy that heals, that restores to value . . . that expresses unshakeable love . . .

My heart feels this steadfast, this faithful love for me as I pray . . .

"Wash me thoroughly . . ." I dare, like David to ask even this . . .

"For I know my transgressions..." I ask the Lord to give me this self-knowledge, the first precious step toward healing...

"Behold, you desire truth in the inward being..." This is the truth I seek: truth in the heart, this truth that you desire, that you love...

"Teach me wisdom in my secret heart..." Make my heart wise in love...

"Wash me, and I shall be whiter than snow." "Make me hear joy and gladness..." I ask this blessed washing, I desire this joy and gladness...

"Create in me a clean heart, O God." I feel the beauty of this "clean heart..." I long for this heart... With simple trust, I ask of the Lord this gift...

"O Lord, open my lips, / and my mouth shall show forth your praise..." A song of praise for new freedom from my obstacles to love...

"The sacrifice acceptable to God is a broken spirit; / a broken and contrite heart, O God, you will not despise." I turn to the Lord, who comes not for the righteous but for sinners (Mk 2:17)...I feel the enfolding embrace of his cleansing love...

After the Prayer

- *What word in this Scripture most spoke to my heart?*

- *What touched my heart in this time of prayer? What did my heart feel as I prayed?*

- *What did I sense the Lord saying to me?*

ZACCHAEUS

Luke 19:1–10

"Make haste and come down; for I must stay at your house today."

Scripture Reading

*As I begin, I become aware of the Lord present to me,
looking upon me with love, desirous of speaking to my heart...*

Prayerfully, I read Luke 19:1–10.

Meditation

I see the crowd, filling the narrow streets of Jericho. I see Jesus in the midst of them, passing through, on his way...

And I become aware of this figure, Zacchaeus, hoping for so little, simply to see the Lord...and unable to do so because of his small stature. He senses all that is wrong with his life, how he is rejected by his own people...and in his own eyes.

I see him move ahead of the crowd, climb the tree...and wait. I am near him, perhaps I take his place...I, too, long to see the Lord: "My heart says to you, 'Your face, Lord, do I seek.' / Hide not your face from me" (Ps 27:8–9). I wait...

And then, like Zacchaeus, I find that it is the Lord who sees me. He stops. He sets aside his journey, he seems almost to forget it entirely in his desire to see Zacchaeus, to see me...

He looks at me..."Zacchaeus, make haste and come down...I must stay at your house today."

I sense the wonder and the joy in Zacchaeus as he realizes the desire of the Lord to be with him. He makes haste to respond... My own heart begins to grasp the desire of the Lord to be with me. I too respond...

Now they — we — are together in the house. What takes place between them? A meal? A conversation? I see Jesus and Zacchaeus together. I am there, with them.

What does Jesus say to him? To me? What does Zacchaeus say to Jesus? What do I share with Jesus about my life, my hopes, my fears, my desire to change?

Zacchaeus is made new...his whole life is filled with a new freshness and a new hope. With courage, the courage of the Lord's presence, the Lord's love, the Lord's words to him, he will make the changes...A new sense of hope fills my heart too...

"Today salvation has come to this house..." *Today*...I hear Jesus' words, I sense the gift offered to me, even today as I pray. My heart responds...

After the Prayer

- *What word in this Scripture most spoke to my heart?*
- *What touched my heart in this time of prayer? What did my heart feel as I prayed?*
- *What did I sense the Lord saying to me?*

GREATNESS THROUGH SERVICE

Matthew 20:20–28

"Even as the Son of man came not to be served but to serve…"

Scripture Reading

*As I begin, I become aware of the Lord present to me,
looking upon me with love, desirous of speaking to my heart…*

Prayerfully, I read Matthew 20:20–28.

Meditation

Now I am about to contemplate the life of Jesus, the events of his hidden and public life. I seek to know God's specific call to me now, how he is calling me to follow Jesus more deeply in the way I live each day. Before I begin, I seek a Gospel sense of *the way Jesus lives:* What does he put in the first place? Which way does he follow? Which way does he set aside? What is he saying to me now through his choice?

I watch as the mother of the sons of Zebedee approaches the Lord, with her two sons. They seek the places of honor, to be "above" the other disciples, to have human status and the honor that accompanies it, to be held in greater esteem than the others… "Command that these two sons of mine may sit, one at your right hand and one at your left, in your kingdom."

It is easy for me as well to wish to be held in honor…

"You do not know what you are asking. Are you able to drink the cup that I am to drink?" I listen as Jesus reveals to them a completely different sense of what is to be sought, of what makes for true greatness in God's eyes…

"It shall not be so among you... Whoever would be great among you must be your servant..."

He asks them, he asks me now, to look profoundly at his life, his choice... and to choose this too: "Even as the Son of man came not to be served but to serve, and to give his life as a ransom for many." To serve... to give...

I turn to the Son of man, the Lord Jesus who loves me, who is here with me now as I pray, and I hear him speak to me of the deep meaning of his life... the one who "emptied himself, taking the form of a servant" (Phil 2:7).

I ask now of the Lord the grace of the true greatness of the kingdom: greatness through humility, through Gospel simplicity of life, through the gift of self in service to others... a difficult way... and the way that leads to true joy. It is the way of Jesus himself.

My heart speaks to the Lord...

After the Prayer

- *What word in this Scripture most spoke to my heart?*
- *What touched my heart in this time of prayer? What did my heart feel as I prayed?*
- *What did I sense the Lord saying to me?*

A VISIT OF SHARING IN THE SPIRIT

Luke 1:39–56

"She entered . . . and greeted Elizabeth."

Scripture Reading

As I begin, I become aware of the Lord present to me,
looking upon me with love, desirous of speaking to my heart . . .

Prayerfully, I read Luke 1:39–56.

Meditation

I journey with Mary, walking with her the days of her traveling, looking upon her, speaking with her . . .

I am present at the meeting of these two women in whom the Spirit is working. . . . I hear the words they share, I sense the deep joy in the Spirit which fills them . . .

Mary journeys "with haste": a desire to assist Elizabeth in her time of need . . . and, perhaps, a personal need to share the mystery of the Child conceived in her womb with the only one who, because of her own experience, may be able to understand . . .

The women speak . . . and both are filled with joy, both are strengthened in the task God has given them . . . I ask of the Lord the gift of such sharing with others in my own life, to be this kind of person for others . . .

"Elizabeth was filled with the Holy Spirit." I ponder what it means to live "filled" with the Spirit, I sense the fascination of such a life, I ask this of God . . .

"Blessed is she who believed..." She *who believed....* I ponder what it meant for Mary to believe in these circumstances of her life. Reverently, I ponder the sentiments and thoughts that fill her heart... A sense of her "blessedness" before God arises within me. I turn to the Lord and speak my desire...

"My spirit rejoices": Does my spirit rejoice? What gives me joy? Diminishes my joy? "My spirit rejoices in God." *In God...* I seek this joy, spiritual joy...

"He has regarded the low estate of his handmaiden." I share with Mary her sense of marvel that God, from on high, has taken notice of her, has looked upon her, has loved her, has called her... And my soul too sees how God has looked upon my low estate... with love, with a call...

I look at Mary, close to her, and I listen with heartfelt attention as she proclaims the words of her Magnificat... I ponder these words, I speak with her about them... I make them mine...

I walk with Mary through the days of her three months of service to Elizabeth. I note what she does, how she does it, when she speaks and how, when she is silent...

After the Prayer

- *What word in this Scripture most spoke to my heart?*
- *What touched my heart in this time of prayer? What did my heart feel as I prayed?*
- *What did I sense the Lord saying to me?*

THE SELF-EMPTYING OF JESUS

Philippians 2:1–11 or Luke 2:1–20

"Have this mind in you which was in Christ Jesus."

Scripture Reading

As I begin, I become aware of the Lord present to me,
looking upon me with love, desirous of speaking to my heart...

Prayerfully, I read Philippians 2:1–11 or Luke 2:1–20.

Meditation

Philippians 2:1–11

I think of Jesus as he comes into the world. Everything begins with an astounding gesture of service, of love, with an emptying of self:

"Though he was in the form of God, he did not count equality with God something to be grasped..."

"but emptied himself..." Jesus, *emptying* himself...

"taking the form of a servant..." Jesus, a *servant*....

"Being found in human form he humbled himself..." Jesus, *humble*....

"and became obedient unto death, even death on the cross..." Jesus, *obedient*....

The "downward" trajectory of the life of Christ, the self-emptying way he follows in bringing about the salvation of the world...my salvation...

His self-emptying is rich with spiritual fruit for the world: "Therefore God has highly exalted him..."

"and bestowed on him the name which is above every other name"

"that at the name of Jesus every knee should bow...and every tongue confess that Jesus Christ is Lord."

I hear his call to share in his way of Gospel simplicity and service...

Luke 2:1–20

In his birth, he chooses humble and poor circumstances, people of little standing in the world: Mary, Joseph, poor shepherds...I am there, present to these events, absorbing the richness of Gospel values they reveal...

"She gave birth to her first-born son...and laid him in a manger...There was no place for them in the inn...Be not afraid...I bring you good news of a great joy...a Savior, who is Christ the Lord..."

"Mary kept all these things, pondering them in her heart." Now my heart, too, like Mary's, slowly ponders "all these things..."

His choice of the way of humble self-emptying speaks to me. Lord, what are you saying to my heart now?

After the Prayer

- *What word in this Scripture most spoke to my heart?*
- *What touched my heart in this time of prayer? What did my heart feel as I prayed?*
- *What did I sense the Lord saying to me?*

CONSECRATED IN THE SPIRIT

Matthew 3:13–17

"He saw the Spirit . . . descending like a dove, and alighting on him."

Scripture Reading

As I begin, I become aware of the Lord present to me,
looking upon me with love, desirous of speaking to my heart . . .

Prayerfully, I read Matthew 3:13–17.

Meditation

I live with Jesus the moment when he leaves all that has been familiar to him for thirty years . . . and, alone, supported only by his trust in the Father's will, sets out to fulfill the mission the Father has given him. I remember my own leaving, my own "setting out" — the setting out to which God continues to call me daily . . .

"Then Jesus came from Galilee to the Jordan . . ." I am there in Nazareth with Jesus. I watch as he senses that the time has come to depart — a man like us in all things but sin (Hb 4:15). I ponder what this parting means for him, for his mother . . .

I journey with him to the Jordan. I speak with him, ask him what he experiences as he sets out alone, unaccompanied, unknown, faithful to his Father . . .

The river, the crowds, the Baptist, the hopes in the people's hearts . . . and Jesus humbly submitting to the rite of John's baptism . . . Water itself is changed and given new power . . . I ponder the mystery of my own baptism, when it took place, how it came to be, what it means in my life . . .

And, slowly, reverently, I witness this powerful moment when the Trinity is revealed...

I see the Spirit descend upon Jesus, anointing him within, consecrating him as the Christ for his mission of redemption. The Spirit — Advocate, Gift of God, Fire, Spiritual Anointing, Love — pours into the heart of Christ... and into mine...

The Father speaks: "This is my beloved Son..." With affectionate awe, I enter the mystery of the infinite love of the Father for the Son, and of the Son for the Father. I discover here the root of Jesus' joy... I hear the Father say to me, made his in baptism: *You* are my beloved son, my beloved daughter...

My heart seeks to grasp, to accept, the mystery of such a love given me...

After the Prayer

- *What word in this Scripture most spoke to my heart?*
- *What touched my heart in this time of prayer? What did my heart feel as I prayed?*
- *What did I sense the Lord saying to me?*

THE FIRST OF THE SIGNS

John 2:1–11

"Do whatever he tells you."

Scripture Reading

*As I begin, I become aware of the Lord present to me,
looking upon me with love, desirous of speaking to my heart...*

Prayerfully, I read John 2:1–11.

Meditation

I am present at the wedding. I see the Mother of Jesus, I see Jesus himself, and the first disciples, the spouses, the crowd, the celebration... I live this whole event, present, watching, listening, contemplating...

This moment is filled with meaning: God, in Jesus, the Word made Flesh, the divine Bridegroom, has come to dwell with, to be wedded to his people...

"They have no wine." Gradually the wine begins to fail... and Mary *sees* the unexpressed need. She seems the first to notice. She shows her profound sensitivity to the human situations and unspoken needs around her, even to the small needs of others... alert, attentive...

Am I like her? Do I see the unexpressed needs of the others with whom I live—needs for help, for companionship, a need to share?

Mary does not simply notice. She becomes active in this situation of need. She becomes *involved*. She brings the need to Jesus, she is engaged to the end, till the need is met.

Do I notice and remain apart? Do I, perhaps too easily, simply assume that I cannot contribute, cannot help?

"O woman, what have you to do with me?" An enigmatic answer, not easy to understand...Yet Mary shows *courage,* she is sure of Jesus. She does not give up, does not say that she has tried in vain...She persists. She knows her Son...

At times I try to help, to improve things...and my efforts seem to meet no response. Do I give up? Do I say that I've tried, but there is no use? Now I ask Mary to speak to me of her courageous and continuing involvement...

I watch Jesus work his first sign, his first miracle...I watch the servants as they fill the jars, the steward of the feast as he tastes the water made wine...

I watch the reaction of the disciples: they see his glory, and faith is born in them...

After the Prayer

- ◆ *What word in this Scripture most spoke to my heart?*
- ◆ *What touched my heart in this time of prayer? What did my heart feel as I prayed?*
- ◆ *What did I sense the Lord saying to me?*

THE SAMARITAN WOMAN

John 4:1–42

"If you knew the gift of God..."

Scripture Reading

As I begin, I become aware of the Lord present to me,
looking upon me with love, desirous of speaking to my heart...

Prayerfully, I read John 4:1–42.

Meditation

I am there by the well...I see the dry countryside surrounding the well, the earthen road...I feel the heat of the midday hours...

I see Jesus seated by the well, alone, his weariness revealed in his face as he rests...I become aware that he is waiting for me, that he has a "gift of God" that he longs to give to me today...

I see the woman approach. I see — perhaps I share — her weariness, her burden of repeated failure: five husbands, over and over the same pattern of failure. I feel her sense of helplessness, of burden, of inability to change...With my own sense of helplessness, of inability to grow as I so desire, I stand there, with her, in her place, before Jesus...

He speaks: "Give me a drink." She does not flee from the conversation that opens so simply...and her life begins to change.

"If you knew the gift of God..." I ask Jesus to help me know the gift that he is offering me even now, as I pray. I ask for eyes that are spiritually open *to see this gift*...and to embrace it in my life.

I watch, I am in her place, as Jesus, gently, and with great respect for the burdens of her heart, unfolds for her the meaning of her own life, and leads her to grasp the gift he wishes to give her: "living water," a new freshness in the power of the Spirit.

Desire for this newness wells up in her, in me: "Give me this water, that I may not thirst..."

Now she becomes a witness to Jesus: "Come, see a man who told me all that I ever did." She has found a Heart before which she need keep *nothing* hidden, before which openness does not wound, but heals...

"Many...from that city believed in him because of the woman's testimony." I ask the Lord that his healing touch in my life make of me too a witness, a channel of his light for others...

I read this passage slowly, I live this passage...

After the Prayer

- *What word in this Scripture most spoke to my heart?*
- *What touched my heart in this time of prayer? What did my heart feel as I prayed?*
- *What did I sense the Lord saying to me?*

* 21 *

"PUT OUT INTO THE DEEP"

Luke 5:1–11

"At your word I will let down the nets."

Scripture Reading

As I begin, I become aware of the Lord present to me,
looking upon me with love, desirous of speaking to my heart...

Prayerfully, I read Luke 5:1–11.

Meditation

I am there by the lakeside, in the morning hour. I see Jesus standing by the water, the crowds, the boats drawn up on the shore. The crowds press upon him to hear his teaching. I mingle with them, I listen as Jesus teaches...

"Getting into one of the boats, which was Simon's, he asked him to put out a little from the land." I draw near...and now I am present in the boat as Jesus and Peter speak...

I am with Peter, perhaps I feel moved to take Peter's place...and I hear the Lord say to me, as to Peter: "Put out into the deep." Put out into the deep! Do not simply continue as you have until now, but *put out into the deep* in your daily spiritual life, in living your calling...

The first request was not difficult: "he asked him put out a little from the land." The second is more demanding: "Put out into the deep..." I ask the Lord to show me where he is calling me to put out anew...to go deeper in my calling...

Peter expresses my own sense of helplessness: "We toiled all night and took nothing!" Months, even years of toil, and the same struggles continue...

But now the moment of grace arrives, the moment of faith, the moment of trusting the Lord's word with courage: "But at your word I will let down the nets." I ask the Lord to give me new courage, fresh trust in his word...so that I may take that new step...

I see the astounding fruitfulness of this simple act of trust in the Lord's word, in the Lord's invitation to "put out" into the "deep": the useless toil is transformed into an overflowing abundance...the nets are filled to breaking, the boats to their utmost capacity...

My life too can change...

Peter, sensing the closeness of God to him in Jesus, senses also his own sinfulness: "Depart..." I cannot be this close to the Divine...

Jesus' answer is immediate: "Do not be afraid." Do not be afraid...I hear him say these words, again and again, to my heart, to my fear...

And he gives to Peter, gives to me, a sharing in his own mission of salvation: "From now on you will be catching men."

They leave all, and follow him...

After the Prayer

+ *What word in this Scripture most spoke to my heart?*

+ *What touched my heart in this time of prayer? What did my heart feel as I prayed?*

+ *What did I sense the Lord saying to me?*

* 22 *

THE COURAGE TO TELL JESUS EVERYTHING

Mark 5:24–34

"Daughter, your faith has made you well."

Scripture Reading

As I begin, I become aware of the Lord present to me,
looking upon me with love, desirous of speaking to my heart…

Prayerfully, I read Mark 5:24–34.

Meditation

I meet this woman. She and I have so much to share: a burden, a need for healing of body, of heart. We have sought healing year after year, made effort upon effort… without effect. The burden remains, it seems even to worsen…

I live with her these endless years of searching for wholeness, for healing… I feel her growing sense of helplessness, her gradual loss of hope… Yet, some small hope remains… and comes alive when she hears of Jesus, and dares to hope that, though him, she may at last find healing.

I watch her, perhaps I take her place, I accompany her, as she comes to the roadside where Jesus is passing. I see the crowds that surround him and hem him in… the movement, the bustle. Now is the chance…

She does not miss the opportunity. She comes close in the crowd. She hopes only for a brief touch of his garments from behind in the crowd. She does touch his garments… and senses that she is healed!

But Jesus wants to give her more. He will not let his "daughter" remain simply an impersonal touch in a crowd. He stops, he asks, "Who touched my garments?"

The disciples cannot understand his question, but he knows, and she knows. ...Now this courageous woman responds. She falls on her knees before him, and "in fear and trembling," tells him "the whole truth."

I marvel at her courage, her trust, her ability to do what I have so often wished to do: to tell Jesus *the whole truth* of what stirs in my heart. Have I anything hidden in my heart that now the Lord wishes me to say to him? I pray for the courage, the trust, the openness that I see in this woman...

Now I hear Jesus call her "daughter," confirming the deep and rich relationship between them...In the silence of my heart, I hear him say this word to me...

"Your faith has made you well; go in peace..." She goes now, her heart in blessed peace...I walk with her...

After the Prayer

- *What word in this Scripture most spoke to my heart?*
- *What touched my heart in this time of prayer? What did my heart feel as I prayed?*
- *What did I sense the Lord saying to me?*

A DAY WITH JESUS

Mark 1:21–39

"They brought to him all who were ill . . ."

Scripture Reading

*As I begin, I become aware of the Lord present to me,
looking upon me with love, desirous of speaking to my heart . . .*

Prayerfully, I read Mark 1:21–39.

Meditation

I am there in the crowded synagogue. I watch as Jesus enters . . . and I marvel as he speaks of God's love, of the great commandment, of salt and light, of the pearl of great price, of a treasure hidden in a field . . . of *good news:* "The people were astonished at his teaching." My heart responds to him, "the light of the world . . ."

Suddenly, an unclean spirit cries out in our assembly . . . and I watch as, with a word, Jesus shatters the power of the evil one: "Quiet! Come out of him!" The man is healed, set free. My marvel grows as Jesus is revealed in power as teacher and healer . . . I turn to him now in my own need . . .

I accompany him as he enters Simon's house. I watch as he approaches Simon's mother-in-law, who lies ill with a fever. I see him grasp her hand and gently help her up . . . and she is healed. I sense the thrill of joy in her heart as she serves those in the house. I ask that I too may "serve the Lord with gladness" (Ps 100:2) . . .

I share the afternoon hours in the quiet, happy, intimate communion of this household gathered around Jesus. I watch him, I listen to him, I speak to him, as my heart desires...

Now it is evening, and the Sabbath rest is completed. I sense the crowd gathering outside the door — suffering hearts, bodies in pain, lives burdened by the oppression of evil. It is my world that gathers there...

I watch as Jesus goes out into the sorrows of the world...my world. I watch him heal with a touch: a paralyzed man walks, a woman stands again, a blind man sees, a young girl rises from her stretcher...Joy bursts forth around me in the crowd. Now, I too stand before the Lord. Our eyes meet...I too ask for his healing touch...

The crowd leaves rejoicing, and Jesus goes to rest. The quiet hours of the night pass...I watch him rise, and I follow him reverently as he goes out alone to pray: "rising very early before dawn, he left and went off to a deserted place, where he prayed."

Now my heart is stilled. I too enter the silence, the mystery of Jesus' heart absorbed in deep and blessed communion with his Father...I turn to him, I speak to him, I ask him for the gift of faithful prayer in my life too.

He goes on to the next village, where others await him. I join him, and ask him to make me the instrument of his healing today...

After the Prayer

- *What word in this Scripture most spoke to my heart?*
- *What touched my heart in this time of prayer? What did my heart feel as I prayed?*
- *What did I sense the Lord saying to me?*

24

A GOSPEL WAY OF LIFE

Matthew 5:1–48

"You have heard that it was said . . . But I say to you . . . "

Scripture Reading
---

*As I begin, I become aware of the Lord present to me,
looking upon me with love, desirous of speaking to my heart . . .*

Prayerfully, I read Matthew 5:1–48.

Meditation

I see the mountainside, I see the crowds, I join them, and sit with them, close to the feet of Jesus. He is seated before me, and he looks at me. He speaks his words now to me, to my heart. All else fades, and I simply listen to his word with all my heart . . . I take one or more prayer periods here . . .

Beautiful words, demanding words, a Gospel way of life, fresh, new, vibrant, challenging, costly, happy . . .

I read, I listen to these words slowly, stopping wherever a word touches my heart, wherever I sense the Lord speaking to me now . . .

The Beatitudes
"Blessed are . . .

"the poor in spirit"

"those who mourn"

"the meek"

"those who hunger and thirst for righteousness"

"the merciful"

"the pure in heart"

"the peacemakers"

"those persecuted for righteousness' sake"

Each of these qualities speaks to my heart. I look at each, and I look at my life in the light of each... I express my desire to the Lord...

Salt, Light, a New Righteousness

Jesus calls me to live in such a way that my life be truly a "salt" of holiness in the world, among those with whom I live; that my life be "light" in this world, leading others to him, the Light of the world.

He speaks to me of a new righteousness, a new holiness, not like that of the Scribes and Pharisees, not linked to the external alone...but in the heart — in authenticity, in sincerity, in genuine love for others...

The Old Way No Longer...

The six antitheses: "It was said...But I say..." I open my heart to each of these, as Jesus speaks to me of this newness:

No anger or insults toward my brother or sister...

A pure heart...

Spousal fidelity...

Total sincerity in my speech...

No longer an eye for an eye...

Love of my enemies...

Lord, what are you saying *to me* today?

After the Prayer

- *What word in this Scripture most spoke to my heart?*
- *What touched my heart in this time of prayer? What did my heart feel as I prayed?*
- *What did I sense the Lord saying to me?*

25

THE WOMAN AT JESUS' FEET

Luke 7:36–50

"She began to wet his feet with her tears . . ."

Scripture Reading

*As I begin, I become aware of the Lord present to me,
looking upon me with love, desirous of speaking to my heart . . .*

Prayerfully, I read Luke 7:36–50.

Meditation

The Pharisee's house, comfortable, well-arranged . . . the room where the dinner takes place, the table in the center, the many guests, the servants bringing food, and Jesus there . . . I read the text slowly, I am there, living each moment of this event.

"A woman of the city, who was a sinner . . ." I see her, alone, scorned, shunned . . . known to be "a sinner." I feel the shame and pain in her heart, her sense of failure. I see how each harsh word, each scornful look cuts deeply . . .

With great respect, I contemplate the stirrings of her heart . . . I sense her overpowering need to find a heart that will not condemn, that will not reject, that will understand the pain and confusion, will perceive the desire to change . . . My heart too knows that great need . . .

She hears of a new rabbi, one who eats with sinners, who chooses to be with the poor and infirm . . . A new hope awakens in her . . . and in me.

She knows that to enter the Pharisee's house uninvited, unwanted, will draw upon her the scorn and rejection of all in the house: "If this man were a prophet

he would have known...what sort of woman this is who is touching him..."
Yet, she draws near...because of her great hope that one heart in that house
will not reject...the same hope that stirs in my heart...

She braves all this...and comes to the feet of Jesus as he, like the other guests,
reclines at the table.

She says nothing. All is said with her actions. Her tears fall...Here I stop, and,
with great reverence, I ponder those tears, their meaning...I look upon her
face, as her tears fall. I look upon Jesus' face, as he sees her tears. What does
she read in his eyes? What do I read in those eyes?

She dries his feet with her hair...she kisses his feet...she anoints them with
ointment...I am there...

And now I hear the words. "Simon, I have something to say to you...One
owed five hundred...the other fifty..." "The one...to whom he forgave
more." "Do you see this woman?" "For she loved much..." "Your sins are
forgiven." "Go in peace..."

I open my heart to hear the Lord speak these words now to me...I speak to
him from my heart...

After the Prayer

- *What word in this Scripture most spoke to my heart?*

- *What touched my heart in this time of prayer? What did my heart feel as I
prayed?*

- *What did I sense the Lord saying to me?*

26

WHY ARE YOU AFRAID?

Matthew 8:23–27

"They came and woke him, saying, 'Lord, save us! We are perishing!'"

Scripture Reading

As I begin, I become aware of the Lord present to me,
looking upon me with love, desirous of speaking to my heart...

Prayerfully, I read Matthew 8:23–27.

Meditation

I am there by the lakeside as Jesus gets into the boat. "And his disciples followed him." This is my heart's desire also — to follow the Lord, to be with him, not to let fear hold me back...

I am with them in the boat as we set out...All is peaceful. I watch as, wearied by his day of service to so many, Jesus, a man like us in all things but sin (Hb 4:15), falls asleep in the stern of the fishermen's boat.

And now, with the disciples, I become aware that the wind is rising, the waves increasing...I watch these fishermen: their words, their faces, tell me beyond doubt that now we are in serious danger...I feel the power of the wind, I hear the crashing of the waves, I see the water pour into the boat...

And I am reminded of the storms in my own life, in the past, now...Suddenly, everything seems out of control, headed toward darkness, ready to give way. ...And I have felt — perhaps I feel now — fear rise in my heart...All human means are exhausted, and the fear remains...

And Jesus sleeps.... I see them draw near to Jesus, as the boat rolls and pitches, tossed by the storm... And, with them, I too cry out: "Lord, save us! We are perishing!" I know this prayer, born of a heart filled with fear...

He awakens, and, *before he intervenes,* says to them, to me: "Why are you terrified, O you of little faith?" I hear Jesus ask this question of me, personally: Why are you afraid? And, slowly, from my heart, I answer. I tell the Lord of the storms in my life, of the storms in my heart, of the fears that burden me...

And I hear his invitation to have faith in him, to trust...

Now, they, and I with them, watch Jesus stand, and, with a word, order the wind and the sea to be calm... With amazement, we hear the wind die, we watch the sea grow calm... We know that all danger is past...

Now I am alone with Jesus. I speak to him of the power I have witnessed in him, of the ease with which he can calm the storms in my life, in my heart... I too marvel at the power in him...

I speak to him from my heart...

After the Prayer

- *What word in this Scripture most spoke to my heart?*
- *What touched my heart in this time of prayer? What did my heart feel as I prayed?*
- *What did I sense the Lord saying to me?*

27

SPEND YOUR LIFE FOR THE GOSPEL

Matthew 9:35–10:16

"When he saw the crowds, he had compassion for them..."

Scripture Reading

*As I begin, I become aware of the Lord present to me,
looking upon me with love, desirous of speaking to my heart...*

Prayerfully, I read Matthew 9:35–10:16.

Meditation

I am with Jesus and his disciples as he travels the earthen roads and the villages of Galilee... I see the crowds flocking to him. I am there as he reaches out to them, teaches them, and heals great numbers of them... I live with him the days of his apostolic mission of mercy...

I look upon his face as he raises his eyes to the crowds, as he senses the burden, the hurt, the confusion, the loneliness of this people. They are "like sheep without a shepherd": no one sees their need, no one heals, no one seems even to notice... This is my world today as well...

I see the deep compassion which stirs in his heart, which moves him to spend his life for them... I ask him for the gift of that same compassion in my heart...

"Pray therefore the Lord of the harvest to send out laborers into his harvest." *Pray therefore....* I hear him say these words to me, asking me to dedicate my life, my prayer, for the many today who are "like sheep without a shepherd..."

I watch him call each one of the twelve, by name, to be part of his saving mission...I hear him call my name now...How do I respond?

"He gave them authority over unclean spirits...and to heal every disease..." I sense the power in him over evil and over all human hurt. I ask him now to share that power with me, that my life too may serve to overcome evil, that I too may be a presence of healing...that I may be his *apostle* in this world...

I look upon each one of these twelve: Peter, Andrew, James, John, Philip...I learn about Jesus, and about whom he chooses...I thank him that he has chosen me...I ask him to renew in me the desire to bring him to this world...

I see him send them out on mission...Two by two, they go out, uncertain, fearful, filled with desire, with trust in his power...I go out with them...to spend my life for the Gospel in the calling God has given me.

Now I listen to his words: Go...preach...heal...live simply...I ask him to explain these words to me...to show me, in the light of this call to proclaim him to others, how I am living today, this year, now...I ask him to help me live these words...

After the Prayer

- *What word in this Scripture most spoke to my heart?*
- *What touched my heart in this time of prayer? What did my heart feel as I prayed?*
- *What did I sense the Lord saying to me?*

28

JESUS SATISFIES OUR HUNGER

Matthew 14:13–21

"And they all ate and were satisfied."

Scripture Reading

As I begin, I become aware of the Lord present to me,
looking upon me with love, desirous of speaking to my heart…

Prayerfully, I read Matthew 14:13–21.

Meditation

I am there by the lake: the boats, the water, the crowds, Jesus, the disciples… and I with them.

News reaches us of the death of the Baptist… Jesus feels the need to be alone … He gets into the boat. The disciples, and I, are with him.

I share with him, with them, this passage across the lake. I look at him, I hear their conversation… I listen, I speak to him…

The crowd sees the boat, thousands hasten along the shore to the place where the boat will land. They come with their need for healing, seeking a new teaching, hoping… I see them, and their great need. I join them, moved by my own great need…

The boat approaches the shore. I see this moment when Jesus first looks upon this great crowd, "about five thousand men, besides women and children."

I see his face in this moment: "and he had compassion on them." A deep stirring of compassion, of love, arises in his heart at the sight of so many in such great need… I feel his response to my own need…

I am there with him, I am there among the people...I watch as he moves through this vast crowd, healing, consoling...I ask for my own healing...

The hours pass, the day is nearly over. Thousands of people, a deserted place, no food...The disciples ask Jesus to send the people away... "You give them something to eat." I sense the disciples' confusion, their failure to understand. ... "We have only five loaves and two fish..." Our human resources are too few for the task. So often I have felt the same...the task seems too great for my ability, my talents...And yet, the Lord asks.

Jesus takes the little they have, blesses it, and gives them *power to feed the whole crowd.* I sense their growing amazement, their awareness of the miracle, of the power in Jesus...They marvel at what they are able to accomplish with his power...

The hunger of the crowd is satisfied. The disciples gather twelve baskets of food that remains. I join them in the task, sharing in their wonder...

Now my heart simply speaks to the Lord...

After the Prayer

+ *What word in this Scripture most spoke to my heart?*

+ *What touched my heart in this time of prayer? What did my heart feel as I prayed?*

+ *What did I sense the Lord saying to me?*

29

WALKING ON WATER

Matthew 14:22–33

"Lord, if it is you, bid me to come to you on the water."

Scripture Reading

As I begin, I become aware of the Lord present to me,
looking upon me with love, desirous of speaking to my heart...

Prayerfully, I read Matthew 14:22–33.

Meditation

I am there, on the other side of the lake. The five thousand have been fed. Now evening has fallen. I hear Jesus send the disciples across the lake in the boat. I see them go... With great goodness, Jesus also sends the five thousand home.

He is alone under the night sky. I watch, I accompany him reverently, as he goes up into the hills. And there, I see him pray... I sense his deep joy in the Father's love, the thrill of mutual love between Father and Son which draws him into prayer, as the quiet hours of the night pass... I watch in silence... and my own heart speaks to the Lord...

The disciples struggle in the boat. The wind and the waves beat against them. I, too, know that struggle against obstacles which make my own progress so difficult... I am there, I see their tired faces, hear their disheartened words. My heart too has spoken such words...

Jesus does not leave them, does not leave me, alone. He comes to them, walking on the water. And they *do not recognize him.* "They were terrified... And they cried out for fear."

He speaks to them, to me: "Take heart, it is I; have no fear." I hear him say these words to me... I listen to these words again and again... I respond...

I see the courage in Peter: "Lord, if it is you, bid me to come to you on the water." I ask this same courage of the Lord, to come to him when I sense his call... to not hold back...

"Come." I hear the Lord say this word to me... I see Peter leave the boat, and begin to walk on water, his gaze fixed on Jesus... And I watch as Peter becomes aware of the wind, of the human insecurity of his position. I sense his courage fail, his fear rise...

He begins to sink... and cries out, "Lord, save me." I, too, have cried out in fear...

Immediately Jesus responds. Two hands clasp: the hand, outstretched in fear, of Peter as he sinks, and the divine hand which holds him up, and saves him, saves me...

"O man of little faith, why did you doubt?" Why do I doubt? I ask Jesus for a simple faith, a great faith...

Jesus and Peter join the others in the boat. The wind ceases. Peace returns. Their hearts lift in adoration. With them, I too say: "Truly you are the Son of God." My heart speaks to him...

After the Prayer

- *What word in this Scripture most spoke to my heart?*

- *What touched my heart in this time of prayer? What did my heart feel as I prayed?*

- *What did I sense the Lord saying to me?*

30

A GLIMPSE OF GLORY

Matthew 17:1–13

"His face shone like the sun."

Scripture Reading

*As I begin, I become aware of the Lord present to me,
looking upon me with love, desirous of speaking to my heart...*

Prayerfully, I read Matthew 17:1–13.

Meditation

"After six days..." Jesus has just told his disciples, for the first time, of the suffering to come (Mt 16:21–28). Now he will strengthen them...and me...to live the time of the cross...

I walk with Jesus and the three disciples. We climb the mount, rising, leaving all else behind...Now there is only Jesus...

With heartfelt affection and awe, we watch as he is transfigured...his face, his garments...The glory of his divinity is revealed, the radiance and beauty of his person...I feel the fascination of the Divine, my heart is drawn to the one I love..."Lord, it is good that we are here..." I say these words, slowly, again and again, to the Lord...These words reveal to me the deepest meaning of my life...

Moses and Elijah speak with him...The cloud of the majesty of God overshadows us...We sense that we are close to the Divine...And in this moment of revelation, I hear the voice of the Father, speaking of the greatest of all loves, the fountain of all love: "This is my beloved Son..."

"Listen to him..." I ask the Lord to teach me how to listen to him, to give me a great desire to listen to him...

"Rise, and do not be afraid..." I hear Jesus speak these words to me today: Rise! Lift up your heart, let spiritual newness enter your life, seek the things that are above...

"Do not be afraid..." Bring to me all your fears... Hesitate no longer... Be filled with new courage...

"They saw no one else but Jesus alone..." I ask that this become reality in my life too: in all the events of my life, in all the people of my life, in my prayer... to see Jesus, to respond to him in all...

They come down the mountain with him... but now all is changed.... I ask the Lord to help me live as one who daily comes down from the mountain, from frequently renewed times of close union with him...

And now my heart speaks freely to the Lord... I share my desires... all that is in my heart.

After the Prayer

+ *What word in this Scripture most spoke to my heart?*

+ *What touched my heart in this time of prayer? What did my heart feel as I prayed?*

+ *What did I sense the Lord saying to me?*

31

FROM DEATH TO NEW LIFE

John 11:1–44

"See how he loved him!"

Scripture Reading

*As I begin, I become aware of the Lord present to me,
looking upon me with love, desirous of speaking to my heart...*

Prayerfully, I read John 11:1–44.

Meditation

A brother and two sisters... and a love: "Now Jesus loved Martha and her sister and Lazarus."

An illness... and a love: "Lord, he whom you love is ill."

I am there as the message of these sisters whom Jesus loves reaches him and his disciples... And for two days he stays there... "This illness is not unto death; it is for the glory of God." My heart begins to speak with the Lord of my own weaknesses, my own fragilities: this illness is not unto death, but for the glory of God. I ask him for new understanding...

"Are there not twelve hours in the day? If anyone walks in the day he does not stumble, because he sees the light of this world..." I sense the Lord's call to "walk in the day" he has given me, this day, this year, this stage in my life.

The disciples fail to understand... Jesus speaks to them plainly: "For your sake I am glad that I was not there, so that you may believe."

Jesus and Martha. "Lord, if you had been here..." My heart too knows this prayer: "Lord, if you had been here..."

She continues: "And even now I know that whatever you ask of God, God will give you..." Her faith strengthens mine. Yes, Lord, even now *I know* that your power can work in me, can change me...

"I am the resurrection...Do you believe this?" I hear Martha's answer of faith...I give my own answer to Jesus...

Jesus and Mary. She hears that Jesus is present and calling her...She rises quickly, she goes to him. I go with her. I too rise quickly to meet the Lord who calls me today...

With great reverence, I am present as these two hearts reveal themselves: "Lord, if you had been here..." Her tears fall..."He was deeply moved in spirit...Jesus wept." I gaze at length upon Mary, upon Jesus, in this moment. I ask Jesus to show me what his heart experiences...

"Take away the stone." The Lord who sets captives free...who sets me free. I ask him to free me from obstacles to new spiritual life...

"Lazarus, come out." "Unbind him, and let him go." With the two sisters, I marvel at the transformation of death into life, at the word of Jesus. I ask him to transform me...

After the Prayer

- *What word in this Scripture most spoke to my heart?*
- *What touched my heart in this time of prayer? What did my heart feel as I prayed?*
- *What did I sense the Lord saying to me?*

32

SUPPER AT BETHANY

John 12:1–8

"And the house was filled with the fragrance of the ointment."

Scripture Reading

*As I begin, I become aware of the Lord present to me,
looking upon me with love, desirous of speaking to my heart...*

Prayerfully, I read John 12:1–8.

Meditation

The Passover is near. Crowds are converging on Jerusalem, in the spring of the year. I am there in nearby Bethany, in the home of Mary, Martha, and Lazarus, as a supper is held for Jesus.

I am there, I watch, I am seated with them. Perhaps, with great reverence, I take Mary's place...

I sense the love here at this table, the deep gratitude in Lazarus, the great love of Martha and Mary for Jesus, his love for each of these three... And the Passover of his Passion is already at hand...

I see Mary choose the most valuable possession she owns, "a pound of costly ointment of pure nard." I sense the desire to give *all* to Jesus revealed by this choice, the love for him that motivates this choice... I speak with the Lord of what my heart desires to give to him...

I watch as she enters, approaches Jesus, anoints his feet with the ointment, and wipes his feet with her hair... I remain here, my heart ponders the meaning of this gesture, I sense the love revealed by the exterior gesture... I glimpse the place that Jesus now has in her heart, how he has become the center of her life...I ask him to enter that deep place in my own heart...

"The house was filled with the fragrance of the ointment." I grasp how her extravagant gesture of love has become a blessing for all those in the house, those with whom she lives...A spiritual fragrance...I ask that my life too become a blessing in this way, for those with whom I live...

An objection is raised against such generous love for Jesus: "Why was this ointment not sold...?"

And Jesus defends her love: "Let her alone..." He loves the generous heart that her gesture reveals. He knows that she has perceived the meaning of the approaching Passover...Her gesture anticipates his death and burial: "Let her keep it for the day of my burial." Love grasps the deep meaning of human situations...

Warmed by the fragrance of her gift of love for Jesus, I speak now to the Lord. I speak of my own desire, my own hope. I ask his grace to love with all that I am...

After the Prayer

- *What word in this Scripture most spoke to my heart?*
- *What touched my heart in this time of prayer? What did my heart feel as I prayed?*
- *What did I sense the Lord saying to me?*

33

"HE LOVED THEM TO THE END"

John 13:1–17

**"Then he poured water into a basin
and began to wash the disciples' feet."**

Scripture Reading

*As I begin, I become aware of the Lord present to me,
looking upon me with love, desirous of speaking to my heart…*

Prayerfully, I read John 13:1–17.

Meditation

Jesus' hour has come… It is the Passover. I see him at supper with the twelve:
the upper room, the food for the meal, the wine…

My gaze centers now on Jesus, in this moment of his self-giving… "Having
loved his own who were in the world, he loved them to the end." "His own." I
thank him that he has called me to be "his own." And I ponder this love, given
to the end: to the utmost degree, to the last moment of his life… given for "his
own," for me…

Now, as I watch, Jesus expresses the whole meaning of his life of service, a life
lived in "the form of a slave" (Phil 2:7), with a symbolic gesture, filled with
meaning…

I see him rise from the table, gird himself with a towel, take a basin with water,
kneel at the feet of one disciple, then another, then another… and wash their
feet… Can I allow him to wash my feet…?

I see Peter resist — he struggles to allow the Lord to kneel before him, to serve him so humbly, to love him in this way . . . I, too, know this struggle . . .

"Lord, do you wash my feet?" "What I am doing you do not know now, but afterward you will understand." How often I, too, do not "know now" what the Lord is doing in my life . . . but later I understand . . .

"You shall never wash my feet." "If I do not wash you, you have no part in me." "Lord, not my feet only but also my hands and my head." Peter allows the Lord to love and serve him . . . I open my own heart to that love . . . and no longer resist . . .

Now I see Jesus take his place again at table . . . I hear him ask me: "Do you know what I have done to you?" Do I know? I answer him . . .

"If I then, your Lord and Teacher, have washed your feet, you also ought to wash one another's feet. For I have given you an example . . ."

I ask the Lord to understand, deep in my heart, his example of service, his love for his own to the end. I share the gratitude for that love which rises in my heart . . . I speak to him now, at length, with profound attention, unhurriedly, from my heart . . .

I ask his grace to love those he has given me to be "my own" with the same love of service . . . to the end . . .

After the Prayer

- *What word in this Scripture most spoke to my heart?*
- *What touched my heart in this time of prayer? What did my heart feel as I prayed?*
- *What did I sense the Lord saying to me?*

34

THE GREATEST GIFT OF ALL

Luke 22:7–30

"This is my body which is given for you."

Scripture Reading

As I begin, I become aware of the Lord present to me,
looking upon me with love, desirous of speaking to my heart…

Prayerfully, I read Luke 22:7–30.

Meditation

Jesus says to Peter and John: "Go and prepare the Passover for us…" All is foreseen, all is carefully prepared for the Eucharist…Nothing happens by chance…I watch Peter and John as they go into the city, as they make the preparations for the meal…I prepare with them for what is about to happen.

Now it is the hour of Jesus…I am there, as evening falls. I see the Upper Room, I see the table, the dishes, the wine, the lamb…I gather with the disciples. Our hearts sense that some great mystery is about to take place…

"I have earnestly desired to eat this Passover with you…" These words open for me the depths of Jesus' heart. I linger here in my prayer, I sense the great desire in Jesus to give the gift of his Eucharistic Body and Blood to his disciples, to me…I speak to him of my desire…

I am there, I watch each detail, each gesture, with profound reverence. I see Jesus take the bread…break it…give it to his disciples, to me…I hear the words: "This is my body…" I realize what this gift has meant, does mean, in my life…I speak to the Lord…

He takes the cup: "This cup...is the new covenant in my blood..." I sense the magnitude of the gift that is given: the gift *of his Body and Blood*, his whole being, to the Church, to me...My heart speaks to him...

Humanity struggles to grasp and accept the gift...One will betray him. A dispute arises regarding who is the greatest among them...And Love is with them, as one who gives himself to them: "For which is the greater, one who sits at table, or one who serves? But I am among you as one who serves."

I become quiet, my soul is stilled. My heart turns toward the Lord, aware of the gift of his Presence, his Body, his Blood, simply gazing, simply receiving, silently giving my own heart. Now, heart speaks to heart, wordlessly, deeply...

"O , you are my God, for you my soul is thirsting..."

After the Prayer

- *What word in this Scripture most spoke to my heart?*
- *What touched my heart in this time of prayer? What did my heart feel as I prayed?*
- *What did I sense the Lord saying to me?*

35

NOT MY WILL BUT YOUR WILL

Matthew 26:36–46

"My Father, if it is possible, let this cup pass from me."

Scripture Reading

*As I begin, I become aware of the Lord present to me,
looking upon me with love, desirous of speaking to my heart...*

Prayerfully, I read Matthew 26:36–46.

Meditation

I accompany Jesus as now he enters his time of sorrow, of burden, the time of the cross...I ask him to show me, through his cross, the meaning of my own sorrows and burdens...

I join Jesus and the Eleven as they walk alongside the city walls toward the Garden of Gethsemane...It is night...I hear the quiet sounds of the night, I feel the heaviness in the hearts of the disciples. My heart too knows times of heaviness and foreboding...

"My soul is sorrowful even to death..." With great reverence, I ponder the sorrow of Jesus, a deep sorrow that nearly overwhelms his life itself...What stirs in his heart? In my heart? I speak to him of my own sorrow...

Now I see Jesus go a little farther into the Garden...and he is *alone.* The three near him sleep. Humanly, he is utterly alone, in his time of need. My heart too knows what it means to feel alone...I speak to him...

His energy fails him...He falls on his face upon the earth, and a cry rises with anguish from his heart, to the Father: "If it is possible, let this cup pass from me…" There is in Jesus a deep, deep desire to be freed of the burden he carries, the burden that lies ahead: "If it be possible, let this cup pass from me…" How often I too have prayed that prayer: *let this cup pass.*… the cup of physical weakness and pain, of responsibility, of struggles in relationships… I am there with Jesus, prostrate on the earth…

"Yet, not as I will, but as you will." Two wills: "as I will," "as you will." And, though it costs his humanity so much, Jesus bows his will to that of the Father… I pray with him, I ask the courage to accept, like Jesus, the Father's will in my life…

He comes, seeking the companionship and support of those close to him… and they sleep… But now I do not sleep… I speak to him…

I watch as, a second time, Jesus repeats his acceptance of the Father's will: "My Father, if this cannot pass unless I drink it, your will be done." And again, a third time… and still he is alone…

"Get up, let us go. Look, my betrayer is at hand." His prayer has strengthened him, he is ready to face the cross… I pray for that same strength…

After the Prayer

- *What word in this Scripture most spoke to my heart?*
- *What touched my heart in this time of prayer? What did my heart feel as I prayed?*
- *What did I sense the Lord saying to me?*

* 36 *

JESUS GIVES HIS LIFE

Luke 23:26–49

"Father, into your hands I commend my spirit."

Scripture Reading

As I begin, I become aware of the Lord present to me,
looking upon me with love, desirous of speaking to my heart...

Prayerfully, I read Luke 23:26–49.

Meditation

The cross...in Jesus' life...and in mine. Now I will accompany Jesus in his supreme moment of self-giving. I ask him for the courage to carry my own cross, to be faithful "to the end," like him.

I join the crowd, pushing through the narrow streets. I see the bustle, the agitation; I hear the clamor, the cries, as we climb toward Golgotha. I see Jesus, scourged, crowned with thorns, condemned, rejected, mocked...carrying the cross, step by step, along the way...

I gaze at him, slowly, with great attentiveness of heart...The image of Jesus carrying his cross penetrates my soul..."If anyone wishes to come after me, he must deny himself and take up his cross daily and follow me" (Lk 9:23). His way of the cross is mine as well...

Simon assists him...What does this moment mean for Jesus? for Simon? The women weep for him. Even now, Jesus is not absorbed by his own pain, but continues to be alive to the need of others: "Do not weep for me; weep instead for yourselves..."

He is *crucified....* I watch the painful stripping; I see the nailing of his hands and feet, the raising of the cross, I hear his tormented breathing...I think of the times when I have felt — or now feel — crucified in some way, stripped of what is dear to me, nailed helplessly in situations of pain...when each day brings its burden, its pain...And I know that I am not alone...

"They will look upon him whom they have pierced" (Jn 19:37). I do this now. I look upon the crucified Lord...and he looks at me. We speak...

"Father, forgive them..." His first thought, his first word on the cross. I linger here, I ponder the forgiveness in the heart of Jesus. I ask for this forgiveness, I ask that forgiveness be my first thought as well...

He is mocked...but one heart turns to him in faith: "Jesus, remember me..." I unite my voice, too, with this prayer..."Today you will be with me..."

Darkness falls, the curtain in the Temple is torn, Jesus cries out with a loud voice: "Father, into your hands I commend my spirit." He gives up his life... faithful to the end. He has given all, now, for me. I thank him...I speak with him of the many "deaths" in my life, the losses, the letting go...

Now, in silence and stillness of heart, I contemplate the one who loved me so much that he gave his life for me...

After the Prayer

- *What word in this Scripture most spoke to my heart?*
- *What touched my heart in this time of prayer? What did my heart feel as I prayed?*
- *What did I sense the Lord saying to me?*

* 37 *

THE WOMEN AT DAWN

Matthew 28:1–10

"I know that you seek Jesus who was crucified."

Scripture Reading

*As I begin, I become aware of the Lord present to me,
looking upon me with love, desirous of speaking to my heart...*

Prayerfully, I read Matthew 28:1–10.

Meditation

The dawn of the first day of the week, the women, the early morning light, the silence, the tomb...The memory of the cross, of Good Friday, the sorrow of his death, are still alive within them...I walk with them, in the quiet of this early hour. What do I sense in their hearts? What is stirring in mine?

We reach the tomb. Suddenly, the earth shakes; an angel, radiant with light, descends from heaven, rolls back the stone...The guards tremble and fall to the earth...Our hearts are seized with wonder and fear...

"Do not be afraid." The first message of the resurrection, the first word to the women...and to me. Do not be afraid...Am I afraid? Can I allow this word to penetrate my heart?

"I know that you seek Jesus who was crucified." These words describe the whole meaning of my life...I ask the Lord that this be increasingly the center of my whole life: "I know that you seek Jesus..."

"He is not here; for he has risen." He is *risen*. I see, I too experience, their struggle to comprehend this word...I sense the dawning of joy in their hearts.

...Death has been reversed, has been overcome...Jesus lives, will live forever. A new hope dawns in my heart too...

"Go quickly and tell his disciples that he has risen from the dead." This is my mission too: to proclaim with my life, my words, my smile, my actions, that Jesus is risen, is alive, is with us, is Lord. I ask Jesus to make of me, too, a witness to his resurrection...

They run, with fear and great joy, to announce his resurrection...

And Jesus meets them, meets us, along the way. "And behold, Jesus met them and said, 'Hail!'" A greeting, and an invitation to joy..."And they came up and took hold of his feet and worshiped him." I share with them this moment of deep reverence and great joy...

"Do not be afraid...go and tell my brethren..." Now I hear Jesus say these words to me: Do not be afraid...Go, and, with your life, your words, tell my brethren...

I speak to the Risen Lord as my heart moves me...New hope awakens within me...

After the Prayer

+ *What word in this Scripture most spoke to my heart?*
+ *What touched my heart in this time of prayer? What did my heart feel as I prayed?*
+ *What did I sense the Lord saying to me?*

38

THE WOMAN IN TEARS

John 20:1, 11–18

"Mary...Rabboni!"

Scripture Reading

As I begin, I become aware of the Lord present to me,
looking upon me with love, desirous of speaking to my heart...

Prayerfully, I read John 20:1, 11–18.

Meditation

I watch Mary Magdalene come to the tomb in the early morning. She sees that the stone has been taken from the entrance...She does not look in, runs to find Simon and John, and returns after they leave the tomb (vv. 1–10).

Now she stands alone outside the tomb. She stands, unable to leave, afraid to look into the darkness of the tomb. Her tears fall...yet still she remains there. I watch with reverence...I seek to understand those tears...I sense that she seems frozen in her sorrow...

I marvel now at her courage: "As she wept she stooped to look into the tomb." *She faces her pain,* her fear: she looks into the darkness of the tomb...and finds that it is not as empty as she feared. A process begins that leads her from her tears to the Lord...

The angels ask: "Woman, why are you weeping?" I hear this question directed to my heart as well: Why are you weeping? Why is your heart heavy as you live day by day?

She sees the "gardener," not recognizing Jesus who is already there with her, even as her tears fall... "Woman, why are you weeping? Whom do you seek?" I answer this question, speaking to the Lord from my heart...

"Jesus said to her: 'Mary.'" Simply her name... I hear him pronounce my name... That one word says everything to me, as it does to Mary...

"Rabboni!" One word... which says everything. She knows now that he is alive, and will live forever, that he is with her, that his love will never leave her, that he calls her by name... She is no longer the woman in tears... I speak now to the Lord. I respond from my heart to his greeting...

The encounter becomes mission: "Go to my brethren and say to them..." "Mary Magdalene went and said to the disciples: 'I have seen the Lord.'" I feel the joy, the delight, the energy, with which she proclaims the risen Lord.

"I have seen the Lord." I speak with Mary Magdalene, I speak now with Jesus, and ask that this too be the central reality of my life, and my message to the world...

Now I sit with Mary. I gaze upon her face, and see there her radiant joy. I see the deep happiness of knowing herself loved, loved infinitely, loved forever... My heart now speaks...

After the Prayer

- *What word in this Scripture most spoke to my heart?*
- *What touched my heart in this time of prayer? What did my heart feel as I prayed?*
- *What did I sense the Lord saying to me?*

39

A JOURNEY INTO HOPE

Luke 24:13–35

"Did not our hearts burn within us while he talked to us on the road?"

Scripture Reading

*As I begin, I become aware of the Lord present to me,
looking upon me with love, desirous of speaking to my heart.*

Prayerfully, I read Luke 24:13–35.

Meditation

I am there, walking with the two disciples. I feel the heaviness of their hearts: "We had hoped..." The energy of the beginnings is past, the time of trial and outward failure has come. They have seen Good Friday...and, now, the tomb...is empty, lifeless.

I walk with them along this country road...I listen to them talk. I see the sadness on their faces. I, too, have known this sadness of a disciple, when all seems to go wrong, when I cannot make sense of what God is doing...

Suddenly, Another is with us. He says little; he simply invites us to share the burdens of our hearts: "What is this conversation...?" "What things?" They pour out their story of a hope that is now passed, of their struggle...

I speak of my own hopes and disappointments...And he listens...

"O foolish men and slow of heart to believe all that the prophets have spoken!" He knows that they — and I — are not "hard" of heart, but only "slow" of heart. Too much has happened, too quickly, and they cannot grasp it in faith, cannot understand it. They falter...

The Listener now speaks to their hearts. He "opens" to them the Scriptures and, slowly, they begin to understand... "Was it not necessary that the Christ should suffer these things and enter into his glory?" "These things" — not the end of hope, but rather the necessary path toward glory...

The "slow" heart becomes a heart on fire: "Did not our hearts burn within us...while he opened to us the Scriptures?" I beg the divine Pilgrim, walking with me through life, for this same burning heart...

"Stay with us..." With them, I make this prayer from my heart to the Lord: Stay with me, Lord Jesus! "So he went in to stay with them..."

We share the meal, the breaking of the bread. And our eyes are opened. Faith flames up, renewed within us. Discouragement is transformed into the surety that the risen Lord is always with me, today, every day, of my life.

Now everything changes for them, for me. They return, with energy, to the heart of the community. And they bear witness to the risen Lord in the midst of others: "They told what had happened on the road, and how he was known to them in the breaking of the bread."

Now I am alone with the Lord. My heart speaks freely to him...

After the Prayer

- _What word in this Scripture most spoke to my heart?_
- _What touched my heart in this time of prayer? What did my heart feel as I prayed?_
- _What did I sense the Lord saying to me?_

40

DO YOU LOVE ME?

John 21:1–19

"They knew it was the Lord."

Scripture Reading

*As I begin, I become aware of the Lord present to me,
looking upon me with love, desirous of speaking to my heart...*

Prayerfully, I read John 21:1–19.

Meditation

I see the lake, the shore, the boats...All is so familiar to these disciples...

"I am going fishing." "We will go with you." So simply...a spirit of harmony, of working together...

Their efforts are in vain...all night...

The day is breaking...In the early morning light, they see a stranger on the shore...They do not recognize him.

"Children, have you any fish?" There is a note of tenderness here...It speaks to their hearts...and mine.

At his bidding they cast the net to the right side...and take in a great quantity of fish...I watch, I sense the beginnings of awareness, the faith that rises in their hearts.

John is the first to understand: "It is the Lord!" This moment of spiritual intuition speaks to my heart. I ask the Lord to open my eyes, to help me to see clearly, to know his presence with me in my work, my efforts, my life...

Peter hastens to the Lord with energy...I sense that nothing will hold him back...

The fire, the meal...their silence. No words are necessary...They know...I live with them this time of silent sharing with the Lord...I too am silent...I too know...

Jesus and Peter...His heart is still bruised by the failure of Holy Thursday evening...I watch as Jesus, with great sensitivity and love, heals Peter's heart. There is no blaming...only a new opportunity to express the deepest reality in his heart...

"Simon...do you love me?" I hear Jesus say my name, and gently ask me that same question: "Do you love me?" I answer...Like Peter, my heart knows that my human weakness does not stand in the way of my answer...

Again the Lord asks...and again...Again I hear Peter's answer....Again I answer...

"Feed my lambs...Feed my sheep." I hear the Lord again entrust to my prayer, to my witness, to my life, the care of those whom he loves, those whom he has committed to my care...And again, I offer myself to the mission...

"When you were young...when you are old..." I allow the Lord to lead in my life...

After the Prayer

- *What word in this Scripture most spoke to my heart?*
- *What touched my heart in this time of prayer? What did my heart feel as I prayed?*
- *What did I sense the Lord saying to me?*

Index

Of Related Interest

Dean Brackley, S.J.
THE CALL TO DISCERNMENT
IN TROUBLED TIMES
New Perspectives on the Transformative Wisdom
of Ignatius of Loyola

As the centerpiece of Crossroad's expanding offerings in Jesuit spirituality and thought, we offer this remarkable book from Dean Brackley, a leader in social justice movements and professor in El Salvador. Brackley takes us through the famous Ignatian exercises, showing that they involve not only private religious experience but also a social, moral dimension, including the care for others.

0-8245-2268-0, paperback

Check your local bookstore for availability.
To order directly from the publisher,
please call 1-800-707-0670 for Customer Service
or visit our Web site at *www.cpcbooks.com.*
For catalog orders, please send your request to the address below.

THE CROSSROAD PUBLISHING COMPANY
16 Penn Plaza, Suite 1550
New York, NY 10001

crossroad

Which Ignatian title is right for you?

Tens of thousands of readers are turning to Fr. Gallagher's Ignatian titles for reliable, inspirational, and clear explanations of some of the most important aspects of Christian spirituality. Whether you're a spiritual director, priest or minister, longtime spiritual seeker, or beginner, Fr. Gallagher's books have much to offer you in different moments in life.

When you need short, practical exercises for young and old:
An Ignatian Introduction to Prayer

Group leaders who are looking for practical exercises for groups, including groups who may not have much experience in spiritual development, will want to acquire *An Ignatian Introduction to Prayer: Scriptural Reflections According to the Spiritual Exercises*. This book features forty short (two-page) Ignatian meditations, including scripture passages, meditative keys for entering into the scriptural story, and guided questions for reflection. These exercises are also useful for individual reflection both for experienced persons and beginners: beginners will recognize and resonate with some of the evocative passages from scripture; those familiar with Ignatian teaching will appreciate the Ignatian structure of the guided questions.

When your life is at a crossroads:
Discerning the Will of God

If you are facing a turning point in life, you know how difficult it can be to try to hear God's will amid the noise of other people's expectations and your own wishes. Ignatius of Loyola developed a series of exercises and reflections designed to help you in these times so that your decision can be one that conforms to God's will for your life.

Discerning the Will of God: An Ignatian Guide to Christian Decision Making is a trustworthy guide to applying those reflections to your own particular circumstances. This guide, which does not require any prior knowledge of Ignatian spirituality, can be used by people of any faith, though some elements will be more directly applicable to Catholic readers.

When you want classic spiritual discipline to apply every day:
The Examen Prayer* and *Meditation and Contemplation

Individuals wanting to deepen their prayer lives using a spiritual discipline will find *The Examen Prayer* an important resource. The examen prayer is a powerful and increasingly popular practice for finding God's hand in our everyday lives and learning to be receptive to God's blessings. This easy-to-read book uses stories and examples to explain what the examen is, how you can begin to pray it, how you can adapt it to your individual life, and what its benefits for your life can be. Highly practical!

A second favorite is *Meditation and Contemplation: An Ignatian Guide to Praying with Scripture*. Anyone familiar with Ignatian spirituality has heard about meditation and contemplation. In this volume, Fr. Gallagher explains what is unique to each practice, shows how you can profit from both at different times in your spiritual life, and reveals some of the forgotten elements (such as the preparatory steps and colloquy) and how the structure can be adapted to your particular spiritual needs.

Because *The Examen Prayer* draws from the experiences of everyday life, it can stand on its own as a guide to the prayer of examen. Those looking to begin their practice of meditation and contemplation, which for Ignatius is always based on scripture, may choose their own scripture passages or draw from the forty examples in *An Ignatian Introduction to Prayer*, mentioned earlier.

When you're ready to move more deeply into Ignatian thought: *The Discernment of Spirits* **and** *Spiritual Consolation*

Spiritual directors, directees, and others who want to understand the deeper structures of Ignatian thought have come to rely on *The Discernment of Spirits: An Ignatian Guide to Everyday Living*, and *Spiritual Consolation: An Ignatian Guide for the Greater Discernment of Spirits*. *The Discernment of Spirits* leads us through Ignatius's Rules for discernment, showing both their precise insight into the human soul and their ability to illustrate the real-life struggles of spiritual seekers today. As Fr. Gallagher writes, his practical goal is "to offer an experience-based presentation of Ignatius's rules for discernment of spirits in order to facilitate their ongoing application in the spiritual life. This is a book about living the spiritual life." Because it forms the foundation for so many other aspects of Ignatian thought, *The Discernment of Spirits* has become Fr. Gallagher's bestselling book and has been the basis for a TV series.

Spiritual Consolation extends this same approach, interweaving stories and principles for a more profound understanding of Ignatius's Second Rules for discernment.

About the Author

Fr. Timothy Gallagher, O.M.V., has dedicated years of his life to an extensive ministry of retreat work, spiritual direction, and teaching in the Ignatian spiritual tradition. He received his doctorate from the Gregorian University in 1983. A member of the Oblates of the Virgin Mary, he has published two books on their founder, the Venerable Pio Bruno Lanteri. He served for twelve years in formation work in this religious community and has taught at Our Lady of Grace Seminary Residence (Boston) and at St. John's Seminary (Brighton, MA); he was also provincial for two terms for the USA province of the Oblates. He currently lives at St. Clement's Shrine, Boston, MA, and is completing a new book for Crossroad on the prayer of examen.